XTREME RESCUES

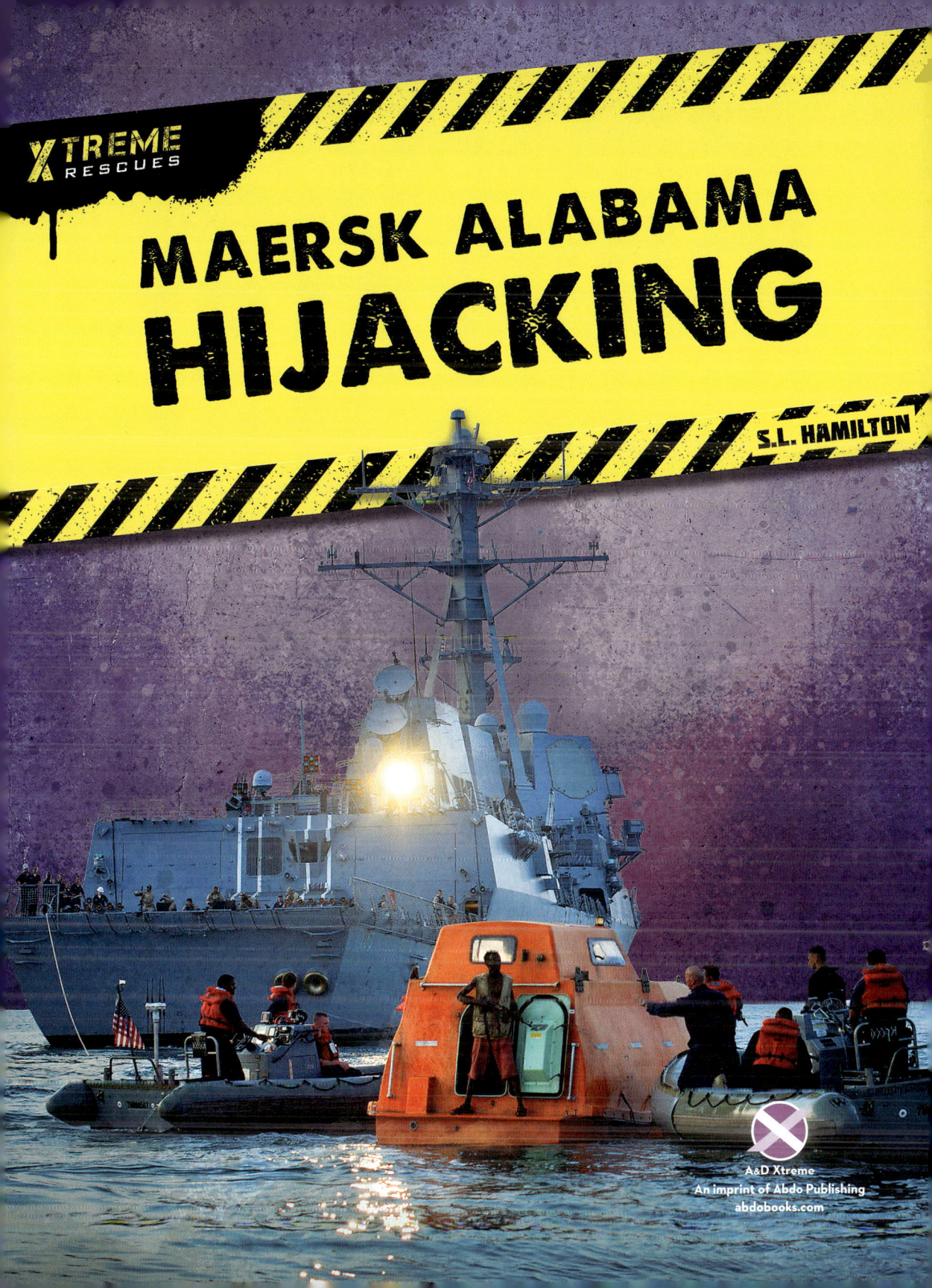

MAERSK ALABAMA HIJACKING

S.L. HAMILTON

A&D Xtreme
An imprint of Abdo Publishing
abdobooks.com

abdobooks.com

Published by Abdo Publishing, a division of ABDO, PO Box 398166, Minneapolis, Minnesota 55439. Copyright © 2020 by Abdo Consulting Group, Inc. International copyrights reserved in all countries. No part of this book may be reproduced in any form without written permission from the publisher. A&D Xtreme™ is a trademark and logo of Abdo Publishing.

Printed in the United States of America, North Mankato, MN.
092019
012020

THIS BOOK CONTAINS RECYCLED MATERIALS

Editor: John Hamilton
Copy Editor: Bridget O'Brien
Graphic Design: Sue Hamilton & Dorothy Toth
Cover Design: Victoria Bates
Cover Photo: Alamy
Interior Photos & Illustrations: Alamy-pgs 1, 8-9 & 12-13;
AP-pgs 2-3 & 4-5; Getty-pgs 14-15 & 16-17;
Sony Pictures-pgs 10, 11, 24-25 & 32;
US Marine Corps-pgs 22-23 & 26-27;
US Navy-pgs 18, 19, 27 (inset), 28-29 & 30-31.

Library of Congress Control Number: 2019942265
Publisher's Cataloging-in-Publication Data

Names: Hamilton, S.L., author.
Title: Maersk Alabama hijacking / by S.L. Hamilton
Description: Minneapolis, Minnesota : Abdo Publishing, 2020 | Series: Xtreme rescues | Includes online resources and index.
Identifiers: ISBN 9781532190032 (lib. bdg.) | ISBN 9781644943519 (pbk.) | ISBN 9781532175886 (ebook)
Subjects: LCSH: Maersk Alabama (Ship)--Juvenile literature. | Hijacking of ships--Juvenile literature. | Maritime piracy--Juvenile literature. | Capture at sea--Juvenile literature. | Maritime operations (Naval forces)--Juvenile literature.

Contents

Pirates Take the *Maersk Alabama* 4
Before the Hijacking 6
Morning Attack 8
Pirates on Board 10
The Crew Fights Back 12
The World Finds Out 14
A Boat and a Hostage 16
The Navy Arrives 18
Escape Attempt 20
Pirates vs Navy 22
SEAL Team Six Arrives 24
The Rescue 26
What If It Happens To You? 28
Glossary 30
Online Resources 31
Index 32

Pirates Take the Maersk Alabama

On April 8, 2009, the loaded cargo ship *Maersk Alabama* was sailing 280 miles (451 km) off Somalia in the Indian Ocean. At sunrise, Captain Richard Phillips and Chief Mate Shane Murphy saw a fast-moving blip on the ship's radar screen.

By 5:30 a.m., four Somali pirates with AK-47 rifles stood on the bridge of the *Maersk Alabama*. They demanded money for the return of the ship. This was the start of five days of terror for Captain Phillips. But the pirates were up against the courage of the *Maersk Alabama* crew and the rescue skills of the US Navy and SEAL Team Six.

XTREME FACT

The Maersk Alabama *was the first US-flagged ship to be boarded by pirates in more than 200 years.*

Before the Hijacking

In the 2000s, toxic waste dumping and drag fishing destroyed the fishing industry in Somalia. Fishermen turned to piracy to make money. Armed with guns, they used their fishing skiffs to hijack and hold ships and people for ransom.

Commandos from Turkey capture Somali pirates. Military ships patrol the Indian Ocean to protect commercial ships, but no one knew when or where pirates would attack next.

Although some sea bandits died while attacking ships, the rare successes made it seem worth the risk. Ransoms quickly rose from thousands of dollars to millions. Piracy became a way to make a lot of money in a short time.

XTREME FACT

In 2007, a total of 12 commercial ships were held for ransom. In 2008, it was 44 ships. In one week In April 2009, 6 ships were attacked, including the Maersk Alabama.

Morning Attack

Just after sunrise on Wednesday, April 8, 2009, a fishing boat raced toward the *Maersk Alabama*. On deck, Captain Phillips saw that the men carried AK-47 rifles. Pirates!

Alarms awakened the crew. They rushed to a secure room while fire hoses shot water around the ship to keep the pirates away. The only guns on board were flare guns. Phillips hoped they could hold off the pirates. The nearest Navy ship, the USS *Bainbridge*, was 300 miles (483 km) away.

Pirates on Board

The pirates matched the ship's speed. They found a place along the side where the water cannons couldn't get them and used a hook ladder to climb aboard. It took only 10 minutes for the pirates to go from being a blip on the radar to walking on the deck of the *Maersk Alabama*.

The pirates use a hook ladder to climb aboard.

A Mayday call reached the Anti-Piracy Command Center in the United Kingdom, but Captain Phillips and two other crew members were already captives of the gun-wielding pirates. The sea bandits cheered when they found out the *Maersk Alabama* was owned by a US company. They thought they would get a fortune in ransom money for the ship and each American on board.

The pirates rush to the bridge of the *Maersk Alabama*.

The Crew Fights Back

The crew knew ways to fight the pirates. Chief Engineer Mike Perry took over the ship using controls located below deck.

A moving container ship's stern shows the powerful waves created by the rudder.

Perry and the first engineer swung the ship's rudder back and forth. This caused waves that made the pirates' boat sink. Later, Perry turned off the ship's power. Only emergency lights remained. To turn those off, Perry snuck forward to the deck and shut down the emergency generator. The ship was now dark.

The World Finds Out

The hijacking of the *Maersk Alabama* quickly became national news. The world learned that a US-flagged ship had been taken by pirates for the first time since the early 1800s. America's response was swift. The destroyer USS *Bainbridge,* the frigate USS *Halyburton,* and the assault ship USS *Boxer* sailed for the *Maersk Alabama*'s location. However, the US Navy ships were at least 14 hours away.

The USS *Bainbridge* is equipped with guns, missiles, and a special radar system that can track more than 100 targets at the same time.

15

A Boat and a Hostage

Pirate leader Adduwali Muse went below searching for the *Maersk Alabama's* crew. Chief Engineer Mike Perry captured Muse at knifepoint. Muse's hand was badly injured. The crew offered to exchange Muse for Captain Phillips. The pirates could have $30,000 cash and leave on the ship's 28-foot (8.5-m) lifeboat. An agreement was made, but the pirates did not keep their word. Phillips entered the lifeboat to show them how to operate it. The four pirates launched the boat with Captain Phillips as their hostage.

A lifeboat similar to the one on the *Maersk Alabama* sits ready to launch.

XTREME FACT

With no power on the Maersk Alabama, *the crew's secure room had no airflow and reached a temperature of 125 degrees Fahrenheit (52°C).*

The Navy Arrives

The USS *Bainbridge* and *Halyburton* arrived on April 9, 2009. The ships circled the lifeboat and launched a ScanEagle drone and a Seahawk helicopter. The pirates were surrounded. They thought other pirates were coming, but none of the other sea bandits wanted to face the US Navy. The lifeboat was 276 miles (444 km) from Somalia. If they reached land, Captain Phillips could easily have been hidden, held for ransom, or killed. The Americans were not going to let the lifeboat get help or reach the shore.

A helicopter flies over the USS *Halyburton* as they check a suspicious boat.

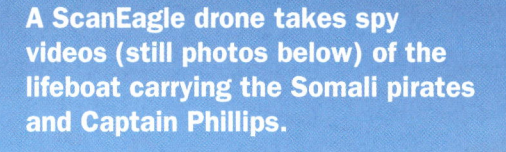

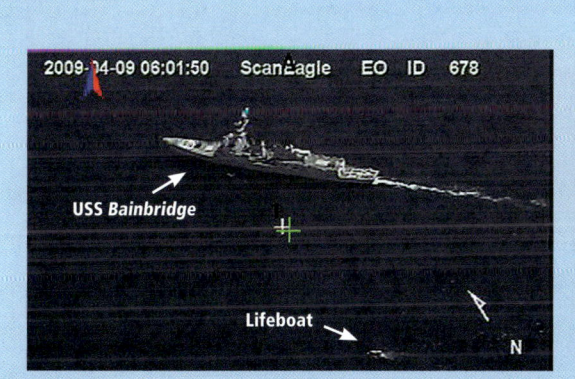

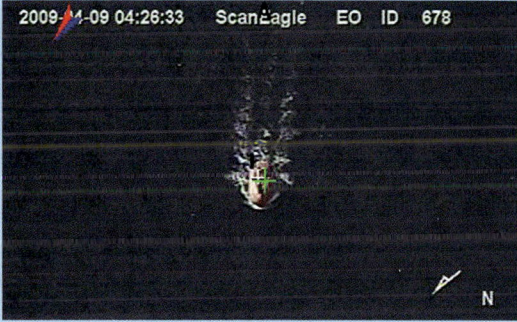

A ScanEagle drone takes spy videos (still photos below) of the lifeboat carrying the Somali pirates and Captain Phillips.

Escape Attempt

Captain Phillips knew the USS *Bainbridge* had arrived. When the pirates were not watching, he dove off the boat and swam for the Navy ship. The pirates immediately fired into the water to get him back. Phillips was tired, thirsty, and hungry. He had been on the lifeboat for 16 hours. The Navy ship was one-half mile (0.8 km) away in rough ocean water.

Water slows bullets, but they can still reach a person underwater. Captain Phillips could have been killed during his escape attempt.

Phillips had to go back to the lifeboat or risk drowning or being shot. The pirates got their prize hostage back. But their excitement would not last. A third Navy warship, the USS *Boxer*, as well as SEAL Team Six, were headed to the area. The pirates thought other sea bandits were on the way, but only tragedy lay ahead for them.

Pirates vs Navy

The Navy harassed the pirates day and night. Loud sirens and superbright spotlights stressed them out. Fire hoses blasted water at the lifeboat, pushing it away from shore.

A Navy patrol plane constantly flew overhead. A Seahawk helicopter used its loud rotors to create hurricane-force winds to keep the lifeboat from moving toward land. The pirates were always aware that they were in deep trouble.

A Seahawk helicopter shows how its rotors can stop a boat in the water.

SEAL Team Six Arrives

After days in the lifeboat, the Somali pirates were hot and seasick. They were running out of gas. Muse and another pirate were injured. They didn't know if the US Navy might attack. No other pirate ships arrived to help them. But far greater problems were coming for the pirates.

Navy personnel use binoculars to keep watch on the pirates and Captain Phillips in the lifeboat.

US President Barack Obama told the Navy to use whatever force was needed to rescue Captain Phillips. With these orders, SEAL Team Six secretly parachuted into the Indian Ocean. A boat from the USS *Bainbridge* quietly picked them up in the dark. Their sharpshooting skills spelled doom for the pirates.

The Rescue

Muse was brought aboard the USS *Bainbridge* to get supplies and medical care on his injured hand. The Navy towed the lifeboat, slowly shortening the tow rope. Now only three people guarded Captain Phillips, and they were within 75 feet (23 m) of the *Bainbridge*. On deck at the stern, 3 SEAL sharpshooters secretly targeted each one of the pirates. No one could be left alive to harm or kill Phillips.

The USS *Bainbridge* towed the *Maersk Alabama* lifeboat after Captain Phillips had been rescued.

The pirates on the lifeboat were getting angry. One pointed a gun at Captain Phillips. Suddenly, a moment came when each SEAL had a clear shot at his target. They fired, killing all three pirates at once. Phillips was brought aboard the *Bainbridge* on Sunday, April 12. After 5 days as a hostage, he was safe. The pirate leader Muse was taken prisoner.

Commander Frank Castellano (left) of the USS *Bainbridge* receives thanks from Captain Phillips.

What If It Happens To You?

Pirates have plundered sailing vessels since ships first sailed the seas. Pirate danger is still real today. Commercial and pleasure ship crews are trained to handle attacks.

Xtreme Fact

The United States does not pay ransom money to kidnappers or hijackers. America will use all of its technology and military might to protect and rescue its citizens.

Should you be on a ship that is fired upon, get below deck and follow the direction of the captain and crew members. Some ships have safe rooms. Pirates usually want to rob passengers or hold the ship or the people for ransom. Many of today's ships can outrun or swamp a pirate ship.

Captain Phillips thanks the crew of the USS *Bainbridge*.

Glossary

Anti-Piracy Command Center
An operation set up to stop piracy and provide security in high-risk areas of the world, such as the Somali coast. The center was in the United Kingdom, but moved to Spain in 2019.

Assault Ship
A US Navy ship, such as the USS *Boxer*, that looks like a small aircraft carrier. They have flat flight decks and carry mostly helicopters and smaller boats.

Destroyer
A middle-sized US Navy surface warfare ship. Modern destroyers, such as the USS *Bainbridge*, usually protect other Navy ships, but have the weapons and technology to strike enemies in water and on land.

Drag Fishing
A way to fish where a ship drags a large net across the seafloor, catching everything in its path. This is usually illegal within 15 miles (24 km) of shorelines as it kills all the fish in an area. Also called bottom trawling.

Frigate
A small-sized US Navy surface warfare ship. Frigates, such as the USS *Halyburton*, are fast and powerful. They are often used to protect other ships, or to stop ships carrying drugs and other illegal cargo.

Harass
To make annoying and hostile attacks over and over against an enemy.

Mayday
A distress signal, usually used by ships and aircraft.

Ransom
Money, or other items of value such as gold or jewels, paid to get something or someone back unharmed.

SEAL Team Six
SEAL Team Six is a supersecret unit of the US Navy that is used on especially dangerous missions. SEALs take their name from the elements in which they operate: sea, air, and land. SEALs are very well trained.

Online Resources

Booklinks
NONFICTION NETWORK
FREE! ONLINE NONFICTION RESOURCES

To learn more about the *Maersk Alabama* hijacking, visit abdobooklinks.com or scan this QR code. These links are routinely monitored and updated to provide the most current information available.

Index

A
America (*see* United States)
Anti-Piracy Command Center 11

B
Bainbridge, USS 9, 14, 18, 20, 25, 26, 27, 29
Boxer, USS 14, 21

C
Castellano, Frank 27

H
Halyburton, USS 14, 18

I
Indian Ocean 4, 6, 25

M
Murphy, Shane 4
Muse, Adduwali 16, 24, 26, 27

N
Navy, US 5, 9, 14, 18, 20, 21, 22, 23, 24, 25, 26

O
Obama, Barack 25

P
Perry, Mike 12, 13, 16
Phillips, Richard 4, 5, 8, 9, 11, 16, 18, 19, 20, 21, 24, 25, 26, 27, 29

S
ScanEagle drone 18, 19
Seahawk helicopter 18, 23
SEAL Team Six 5, 21, 25, 26, 27
Somalia 4, 6, 18

T
Turkey (country) 6

U
United Kingdom 11
United States 5, 11, 14, 25, 28